Ghanaian Favourite Recipe

Advance

Dr. Kwame Pongo

Homecoming Africa Series

Published by:

HOMECOMING AFRICA INC

Website: WWW.HOMECOMING-AFRICA.COM

Email: Info@homecoming-africa.com

Tel: 1 513-848-4547

U.S.A

COPYRIGHT@ 2024

Author:

Dr. Kwame Pongo

ISBN: 9789694290050

DEDICATION

This book is dedicated to my parents, family, and friends for
feeding and teaching me how to prepare all these favorite Ghanaian dishes.
To God be the Glory!!!

Table of Contents

ACKNOWLEDGEMENT

My upbringing was set on enjoying some of the best Ghanaian dishes. My parent's insistence on the family enjoying home-cooked meals hooked me up to these dishes. Growing up in a compound house in Nima gave me the advantage of enjoying other recipes from other parts of Ghana.

The community and primary school vendors did add to my collection. Thanks to my dedicated high school kitchen staff. Spending holidays with my extended family and our men's cooking adventures did help in my perfection of the preparation of these favorite dishes. Spending years in the United States, where the craving for these dishes was so intense, I had no option but to continue to cook some of these dishes. The overwhelming appreciation my workers and group of friends showed me to start writing down these recipes, which I shared with them.

My sincere thanks go to my wife, children, family, and friends, who motivated me on this project and want to see me do more. To all my staff, clients, students, educators, families, and those ready to try these new recipes from Ghana and Africa, I say Ayeeko!!! God richly bless you all.

PREFACE

Thank you for patronizing our products and services. This book is part of our total package to promote diversity and good, natural, nutritious meals from Ghana. We aim to take students, educators, families, and groups to Ghana, West Africa, on this recipe adventure. Our series serves Ghanaians, Africans, and our International families and friends. Though the ingredients are similar, the steps to preparing these dishes make them unique. Learning, cooking, and enjoying new and healthy African dishes from Ghana is never too early.

We started with our beginner's series, where we took our young ones on a journey to experience the best Ghanaian dishes through naming, picture identification, drawing, and coloring.

Our intermediate series gave a breakdown of the key ingredients used to prepare selected best Ghanaian dishes. Activities include identification, drawing, and creating their own favorite dish. The advanced series (Students Work Book and Teachers Guide) gives students, educators, families, and groups hands-on experience preparing and enjoying selected best Ghanaian dishes.

At Homecoming Africa, we are here to ensure you have the whole experience, so you can always reach out to us for further support to maximize your knowledge regarding the best Ghanaian recipes. We also have consultants and experts who will provide face-to-face or virtual presentations on preparing and enjoying the best Ghanaian recipes. Audiovisuals and other teaching and learning materials are also available at your request. We also have the unique ingredients prepackaged for your convenience. We encourage a healthy cooking contest among classes, schools, families, and groups. We hope you will incorporate these dishes into your line of dishes served at schools, homes, and other events. Please share your experiences and feedback to enable us to best serve you.

STEPS FOR ABOBI TADI (ANCHOVI WITH PEPPER)

1. CLEAN THE ABOBI.

2. PLACE IN A SAUCEPAN.

3. APPLY MEDIUM HEAT.

4. CONTINUE TO STIR UNTIL COOKED.

5. WASH PEPPER, ONION AND TOMATOES.

6. GRIND PEPPER, ONION AND TOMATOES.

7. ADD ABOBI (ANCHOVY) TO THE HOT PEPPER.

6. SERVE ABOBI TADI WITH HOT AKPLE OR BANKU.

STEPS FOR ABOLO

1. CLEAN MAIZE BY PICKING BAD AND MOULD.

2. WASH IN CLEAN WATER.

3. GRIND INTO SMALL GRITS.

4. WASH GRITS IN CLEAN WATER TO FURTHER REMOVE THE CHAFF.

5. MIX MASHED GRITS WITH FLOUR AND ALLOW TO STAND FOR ONE HOUR.

6. MIX THE MIXTURE INTO A FINE TEXTURE.

7. DIVIDE THE FINELY MILLED FLOUR INTO TWO PARTS.

8. ADD THE WHEAT FLOUR AND MIX WELL.

9. FETCH AND WRAP THE SOFT PASTE IN CLEAN LEAVES.

10. ARRANGE IN A STEAMER AND STEAM FOR SOME FEW MINUTES.

11. REMOVE FROM STEAMER AND SERVE WITH PEPPER AND FRIED FISH.

STEPS FOR AKPLE

1. GRIND DRY CORN INTO A SMOOTH POWDER.

2. BOIL WATER IN A SAUCEPAN AND ADD SALT TO TASTE.

3. FETCH SOME HOT WATER AND SET ASIDE.

4. PREMIX SOME CORN FLOUR WITH WARM WATER.

5. POUR MIXTURE INTO THE BOILING WATER IN THE SAUCEPAN AND STIR.

6. POUR DESIRED AMOUNT OF CORN FLOUR INTO THE PORRIDGE ON FIRE AND CONTINUE TO STIR WITH A WOODEN SPATULA TO AVOID LUMPS.

7. USING YOUR SPATULA, CONTINUE TO STIR THE MIXTURE TO ENSURE THERE ARE NO LUMPS IN THE PASTE.

8. IF THE PASTE IS TOO WATERY, ADD MORE CORN FLOUR TO ENSURE YOU GAIN THE DESIRED TEXTURE.

9. CONTINUE STIRRING UNTIL THE PASTE HAS THE DESIRED TEXTURE.

10. ALLOW THE PASTE TO COOK BY ADDING SOME HOT WATER AND ALLOWING IT TO BOIL.

11. USE THE SPATULA TO MIX UNTIL AKLPE IS WITHOUT LUMPS AND WELL COOKED.

12. MOULD AKPLE INTO SERVING BOWLS.

13. ENJOY YOUR AKPLE WITH ABOBI TADI, HOT PEPPER AND FISH OR SOUP OF YOUR CHOICE.

1. WASH, BOIL AND COOK THE PALM NUTS IN A SAUCEPAN.

2. ADD WATER AND ALLOW TO BOIL FOR ABOUT AN HOUR.

3. CHECK IF THE COAT OF THE PALM NUT SLIPS OFF THE NUT WHEN RUBBED WITH YOUR FINGERS (THAT MEANS IT'S READY).

4. POUND THE PALM NUTS, ADD WATER AND SIEVE BY SEPARATING THE CHAFF AND NUTS FROM THE LIQUID AFTER YOU HAVE ADDED THE WATER.

5. ADD TOMATO, ONIONS AND PEPPER. LEAVE THE MIXTURE TO COOK FOR SOMETIME.

6. BLEND THE INGREDIENTS AND ADD TO THE MIXTURE ON FIRE.

7. ADD CRABS AND HERRINGS.

8. PUT ANOTHER SAUCEPAN ON FIRE AND POUR SOME OF THE PALMNUT SOUP INTO IT.

9. POUR THE ROASTED CORNFLOUR INTO THE PALM NUT SOUP AND STIR CONSISTENTLY WITH A SPATULA.

10. KEEP STIRRING UNTIL THE PASTE IS WELL COOKED.

11. DISH PORTIONS INTO BOWLS, GARNISH WITH CRABS AND SERVE HOT.

1. CRUSH CORN THEN SOAK IN WATER FOR 3 DAYS (IN ORDER TO FERMENT THE CORN).

2. POUR FERMENTED CORN INTO A SAUCEPAN WITH ENOUGH WATER AND BOIL FOR 30-40MINS.

3. POUR SUGAR IN A SAUCEPAN.

4. STIR CONTINUOUSLY UNTIL IT TURNS DARK BROWN WHICH BECOMES THE SUGAR SYRUP.

5. USING A SIEVE, STRAIN WATER FROM THE BOILED CORN.

6. ADD AN AMOUNT OF THE SUGAR SYRUP TO THE BOILED STRAINED CORN WATER TO YOUR DESIRED TASTE.

7. IF A CHAFF DEVELOPS, STRAIN THE CHAFF WITH A CLEAN CLOTH AND STORE IN A FRIDGE.

8. PUT YOUR ASAANA INTO A GLASS WITH ICE CUBES OR MILK.

9. ENJOY YOUR NATURAL REFRESHING ASANAA DRINK CHILLED.

1. PEEL CASSAVA AND GRATE INTO A BOWL.

2. LEAVE THE GRATED CASSAVA TO FERMENT FOR A DAY OR TWO.

3. SQUEEZE THE GRATED CASSAVA TO REMOVE THE STARCH FROM IT AND ALLOW IT TO DRY.

4. STEAM THE GRATED CASSAVA AND AFTERWARDS SEPARATE TILL IT BECOMES GRAINS.

5. MIX ATSEKE AND WATER IN A BOWL.

6. STEAM THE ATSEKE AND SERVE HOT.

7. SERVE ATSEKE WITH HOT PEPPER AND FISH WITH VEGETABLES (STIR FRIED).

1. MIX CORN DOUGH WITH WATER IN A BOWL.

2. USING A COLANDER AND ANOTHER BOWL STRAIN THE CORN JUICE OFF ITS CHAFF.

3. PUT A SAUCEPAN AND WATER ON A MEDIUM-HEAT FIRE. POUR IN THE CORN JUICE WHEN THE WATER GETS WARM AND STIR. ADD SALT TO TASTE.

4. USING A WOODEN SPATULA, CONTINUE TO STIR THE CORN JUICE TILL YOU HAVE A THICK DOUBLE CREAM CONSISTENCY.

5. ENJOY WITH MILK, SUGAR, GROUNDNUT AND BREAD.

STEPS FOR AYOYO SOUP AND STEW

1. CHOP THE AYOYO LEAVES INTO SMALLER PIECES.
2. CHOP ONIONS INTO SMALLER PIECES.
3. BOIL WATER UNDER HIGH HEAT.
4. ADD CHOPPED ONIONS, POWDERED FISH AND DAWADAWA.
5. AFTER 5-7 MINUTES, ADD AYOYO LEAVES AND SALT PETRE.
6. STIR CONTINUOUSLY UNTIL INGREDIENTS BECOME VERY SOFT(DO NOT COVER).
7. BLEND ONIONS, GARLIC, AND GINGER AND ADD TO MEAT.
8. SIMMER THE CHOPPED MEAT OVER MEDIUM HEAT.
9. ADD SALT AND SEASONING AND COVER. STEAM FOR ABOUT 10MINS.
10. HEAT SAUCEPAN OVER MEDIUM HEAT UNTIL HOT AND ADD VEGETABLE OIL.
11. ADD MEAT TO THE HOT OIL.
12. FRY UNTIL ALL SIDES ARE EQUALLY BROWN.
13. TRANSFER IT INTO A BOWL AND SET ASIDE.
14. ADD CHOPPED ONION TO HEATED PALM OIL IN A SAUCEPAN ON FIRE.
15. ADD GRINDED PEPPER, TOMATOES PUREE AND STIR INTERMITTENTLY.
16 . WASH FISH AND ADD TO THE STEW.
17. ADD SPICES AFTER 10MINS AND ALLOW TO COOK.
18. ADD SALT TO TASTE.
19. ADD FRIED MEAT AND ALLOW TO SIMMER.
20. SERVE WITH TUO ZAAFI, AYOYO AND STEW.

1. MIX 2 PARTS OF CORN DOUGH WITH 1 PART CASSAVA DOUGH WITH ENOUGH WATER IN A POT.

2. ADD SALT TO TASTE.

3. PLACE THE POT ON THE STOVE AT MEDIUM HEAT AND STIR. CONTINUOUSLY TO AVOID LUMPS WITH THE HELP OR USE OF A WOODEN SPATULA.

4. AS THE PORRIDGE COOKS, THE PORRIDGE WILL THICKEN TILL IT COMES TOGETHER.

5. DRIVE BANKU UNTIL DESIRED SOFTNESS IS ACHIEVED.

6. AT THIS POINT THE BANKU IS READY.

7. SERVE WITH SOUP OF YOUR CHOICE OR HOT PEPPER AND FISH.

STEPS FOR EKUAGBEME (CORN GRITS PORRIDGE)

1. WASH THE KERNEL AND SOAK OVERNIGHT.

2. BOIL IT ABOUT AN HOUR.

3. ALLOW IT TO SIMMER AND THICKEN AS PREFERRED.

4. ADD A PINCH OF SALT AND COOK FOR 10 MINUTES.

5. ENJOY EKUAGBEME WITH SUGAR, MILK AND ROASTED GROUNDNUT.

1. CLEAN FISH.

2. SEASON WITH SPICES.

3. HEAT-UP OIL.

4. DROP THE FISH IN THE HOT OIL.

5. FRY UNTIL GOLDEN BROWN.

6. FRY FISH TO YOUR DESIRED TEXTURE.

7. ENJOY FRIED FISH WITH KENKEY, BANKU, OR WAAKYE.

1. PEEL PLANTAIN.

2. SLICE INTO PIECES.

3. WASH IN SALT SOLUTION.

4. POUR OIL IN SAUCEPAN.

5. HEAT OIL.

6. ADD PLANTAINS TO THE HOT OIL ON FIRE.

7. DEEP FRY UNTIL GOLDEN BROWN.

8. SERVE FRIED PLANATAIN WITH YOKE GARI, WAAKYE OR JOLLOF RICE.

1. PEEL POTATOES AND CUT THEM INTO SHAPES.

2. RINSE THE POTATOES, ADD INTO A POT WITH SALT SOLUTION.

3. PLACE A FRYING PAN ON MEDIUM HEAT, ADD OIL INTO THE PAN AND HEAT.

4. ADD THE POTATOES TO THE OIL AND FRY TILL GOLDEN BROWN AND CRISPY.

5. SERVE FRIED POTATOES WITH PEPPER AND FISH.

STEPS FOR FRIED YAM (CHIPS)

1. PEEL YAM AND CUT THEM INTO SHAPES.

2. . RINSE YAM IN SALT SOLUTION.

3. PLACE A FRYING PAN ON MEDIUM HEAT, ADD OIL INTO THE PAN AND HEAT.

4. ADD THE YAM TO THE OIL AND FRY TILL GOLDEN BROWN AND CRISPY.

5. SERVE FRIED YAM WITH PEPPER AND FRIED FISH.

STEPS FOR FUFU

1. PEEL THE SKIN OF THE CASSAVA AND PLANTAIN WITH A KNIFE.

2. CUT THE PEELED TUBER INTO SMALL CUBES AND WASH THOROUGHLY.

3. FILL THE POT WITH ENOUGH WATER TO COVER THE CASSAVA AND PLANTAIN.

4. BOIL CASSAVA AND PLANTAIN UNTIL TENDER.

5. DRAIN WATER.

6. POUND CASSAVA AND PLANTAIN IN A MORTAR WITH A PESTLE TO FORM A DOUGH

7. COMBINE THE CASSAVA AND PLANTAIN DOUGH UNTIL YOUR DESIRED TEXTURE.

8. MOULD FUFU INTO PORTIONS.

9. SERVE FUFU WITH LIGHT SOUP, PALM NUT SOUP OR GROUNDNUT SOUP BY POURING THE SOUP ON TOP OF THE FUFU.

STEPS FOR GARDEN EGG STEW

1   WASH AND CHOP PEPPER, TOMATOES, ONIONS, OTHER VEGETABLES.

2.   BLEND THE INGREDIENTS UNTIL SMOOTH.

3.   HEAT-UP PALM OIL IN A SAUCEPAN.

4.   ADD SLICE OF ONION AND ALLOW TO FRY UNTIL IT TURNS GOLDEN BROWN.

5.   ADD THE BLENDED MIXTURE.

6.   ADD BLENDED COOKED GARDEN EGGS AND STIR TO ALLOW IT MIX PROPERLY.

7.   ADD SPICES AND VEGETABLES.

8.   ADD CHOICE OF FISH OR STEAMED MEAT AND ALLOW TO COOK.

9.   REDUCE HEAT AND ALLOW TO SIMMER.

10.   SERVE GARDEN EGG STEW WITH AMPESI OR PLAIN RICE.

1. CHOP YOUR TOMATOES, ONIONS AND GREEN PEPPER ON TO A PLATE AND SET ASIDE.

2. POUR SOME COOKING OIL INTO A PAN.

3. ADD DICED ONION AND TOMATOES.

4. ADD PEPPER AND SPICES.

5. ADD GREEN PEPPER.

6. ADD SALT TO TASTE.

7. ADD FRESH EGGS.

8. ALLOW STEW TO COOK.

9. WET GARI WITH LITTLE WATER.

10. MIX GARI WITH STEW.

11. SERVE GARI FORTOR WITH MEAT OR FISH.

STEPS FOR GARI SOAKINGS

1. POUR YOUR PREFERRED AMOUNT OF GARI INTO A BOWL.

2. ADD SUGAR, AND WATER.

3. CREAM WITH MILK.

4. ENJOY GARI SOAKINGS WITH ROASTED GROUNDNUT (PEANUT).

STEPS FOR GRILLED TILAPIA

1. CLEAN YOUR TILAPIA, DESCALE IT AND SPICE IT WITH YOUR PREFERRED NATURAL SPICE.

2. LEAVE FOR SOME TIME FOR FISH TO BE WELL SEASONED.

3. THEN PUT THE FISH ON THE HOT GRILL.

4.   FROM TIME TO TIME, BE GLAZING THE FISH WITH OIL AND TURNING AS AND WHEN NEEDED, SO AS NOT TO GET STUCK ON THE GRILL AND GET WELL COOKED.

5. KEEP GLAZING AND TURNING INTERMITTENTLY.

6. ENJOY YOUR TILAPIA WITH BANKU, KENKEY AND SOME PEPPER.

1. CUT UP THE CHICKEN, FISH, OR MEAT AND STEAM WITH GARLIC, ONION, SALT AND GINGER.

2. POUR SOME WATER INTO A SAUCEPAN AND ADD GROUNDNUT PASTE. MIX IT UP TILL ITS CONSISTENT.

3. PUT IT ON MEDIUM HEAT AND STIR UNTIL IT THICKENS WITH THE GROUNDNUT OIL ON TOP OF THE MIXTURE. GET IT OFF THE FIRE.

4. ADD SOME WATER TO THE PREPARED MIXTURE TO MAKE WATERY.

5. PUT THE STEAMED PROTEIN OF CHOICE ON FIRE AND STRAIN THE MIXTURE INTO IT AND BOIL.

6. ADD SOME TOMATOES, ONION AND PEPPER AND BLEND.

7. POUR IT BACK INTO THE BOILING SOUP AND ADD SPICE OF CHOICE AND SALT TO TASTE.

8. ALLOW TO BOIL SLOWLY FOR ABOUT 20 MINUTES AND YOUR SOUP IS READY.

9. SERVE GROUNDNUT SOUP WITH BANKU, FUFU, KOKONTE OR RICE BALLS.

STEPS FOR HAUSA BEER DRINK (LAMUGEE)

1.   SOAK RICE OVERNIGHT TO SOFTEN IT.

2.   THE NEXT DAY, WASH AND RINSE WITH WATER.

3.   POUR THE RICE IN A BLENDER, THEN ADD GINGER, CLOVES AND WATER.

4.   BLEND MIXTURE UNTIL A SMOOTH MIXTURE IS OBTAINED.

5.   SIEVE MIXTURE WITH A FINE MESH. ADD SUGAR AND VANILLA ESSENCE.

6 .   SERVE NATURAL HAUSA BEER (LAMUGEE) CHILLED.

STEPS FOR HAUSA KOKO (PORRIDGE)

1. PLACE MILLET DOUGH INTO A MEDIUM POT.

2. ADD 1 CUP OF COLD WATER AND CRUMBLE UP MILLET DOUGH TO MAKE A SMOOTH PASTE.

3. PLACE OVER HIGH HEAT AND BRING TO SIMMER , STIRRING OCCASIONALLY.

4. ADD 2 CUPS OF BOILING WATER TO PUT AND BRING TO A BOIL, STIRRING CONTINUOUSLY.

5. ADD A PINCH OF SALT, GROUND CLOVES, GINGER AND CHILI POWDER.

6. STIR AND ALLOW TO SIMMER FOR SOME TIME.

7. WHEN READY TO SERVE ADD DESIRED AMOUNT OF SUGAR AND STIR.

8. SERVE WITH KOOSE OR GROUNDNUT.

1. WASH PEPPER, TOMATOES AND ONIONS.

2. GRIND PEPPER, ONION AND TOMATOES.

3. ADD SALT TO TASTE.

4. ADD SLICE ONIONS.

5. SERVE WITH KENKEY, BANKU OR AKPLE.

STEPS FOR ICE KENKEY (MASHED KENKEY)

1. PEEL THE KENKEY AND BREAK INTO PIECES.

2. BLEND BY ADDING WATER AND ALLOW TO MIX UNIFORMLY..

3. POUR INTO A BOWL OR CUP.

4. ADD SUGAR TO TASTE.

5. SERVE ICE KENKEY CHILLED WITH MILK AND ROASTED GROUNDNUTS.

STEPS FOR JOLLOF RICE

1. ADD THE TOMATOES, PEPPER, ONION INTO A BLENDER AND BLEND UNTIL SMOOTH.

2. STEAM YOUR CHOICE OF MEAT WITH NATURAL SPICES.

3. DEEP FRY YOUR MEAT AND SET ASIDE.

4. HEAT YOUR BLENDED VEGETABLES AND SPICES IN VEGETABLE OIL.

5. WASH YOUR RICE IN WATER AND ADD TO THE MIXTURE ON THE FIRE.

6. STIR AND ADD SOME WATER AND ALLOW TO COOK.

7. ADD SALT TO TASTE, STIR INTERMITTENTLY AND COVER THE POT.

8. PREPARE A STEW WITH PART OF THE BLENDED MIXTURE AND ADD YOUR MEAT.

9. STEAM YOUR VEGETABLES OR PREPARE A SALAD.

10. SERVED THE COOKED JOLLOF RICE WITH STEAMED VEGETABLES OR SALAD STEW AND MEAT, HOT.

STEPS FOR KELEWELE

1. USING A SHARP KNIFE, PEEL THE RIPPED PLANTAINS.

2. CUT PLANTAINS IN TO DIAGONAL PIECES AND SET ASIDE.

3. BLEND ONION, GARLIC, GINGER AND PEPPER.

4. POUR BLENDED MIXTURE INTO A BOWL.

5. IN A LARGE BOWL, MIX THE PLANTAIN PIECES AND THE BLENDED MIXTURE TOGETHER.

6   LET IT REST FOR ABOUT 10-20 MINS TO ABSORB THE FLAVOR.

7. HEAT UP A LARGE PAN WITH OIL FOR DEEP FRYING UNDER HIGH MEDIUM HEAT UNTIL HOT.

8. FRY THE PLANTAIN PIECES UNTIL GOLDEN BROWN.

9. REMOVE AND TRANSFER INTO A SIEVE FOR DRAINAGE OF OIL.

10. SERVE KELEWELE WARM WITH ROASTED GROUNDNUT.

STEPS FOR KENKEY

1. PUT HALF OF THE CORN DOUGH IN A BOWL AND MIX WITH WATER.

2. BOIL CORN DOUGH UNTIL HALF WAY COOKED.

3. SPREAD THE DOUGH ON A LARGE CLEAN SAUCEPAN AND ADD THE REMAINING RAW CORN DOUGH USING A WOODEN LADLE.

4. MIX TOGETHER THOROUGHLY.

5. MOLD INTO PREFERRED SIZES.

6. WRAP EACH WITH THE CORN HUSKS.

7. PLACE SOME CORN HUSKS AT THE BOTTOM OF A BIG SAUCE PAN AND ARRANGE THE WRAPPED DOUGH NICELY ON IT.

8. ADD ENOUGH WATER, COVER AND BOIL FOR ABOUT 10MINUTES.

9   KENKEY IS READY.

10. SERVE WITH HOT PEPPER AND FISH.

1. PLACE WATER IN A POT AND BRING TO BOIL.

2. SET ASIDE PART OF THE HOT WATER.

3. ADD THE KOKONTE FLOUR TO THE BOILING WATER ON FIRE.

4. STIR CONTINUOUSLY TO AVOID THE MIXTURE FORMING LUMPS.

5. PRESS THE MIXTURE AGAINST THE SIDE OF THE POT WITH A LADLE.

6. ADD EXTRA HOT WATER AND COVER IT TO COOK FOR SOMETIME.

7. REMOVE COVER AND CONTINUE TO STIR UNTIL SOFT AND WELL COOKED.

8. SERVE INTO PORTIONS.

9. ENJOY KOKONTE WITH YOUR CHOICE OF SOUP OR HOT PEPPER AND FISH.

STEPS FOR KOOSE

1. PREPARE THE BEANS BY SOAKING AND DE-HULLING 2 DAYS IN ADVANCE.

2. PLACE THE BEANS INTO A BLENDER AND BLEND.

3. ADD THE ONIONS, GINGER AND PEPPER TO THE BLENDER.

4. BLEND UNTIL SMOOTH.

5. ADD SALT.

6. HEAT UP THE COOKING OIL IN A SAUCEPAN.

7. USING A TABLESPOON, SCOOP MIXTURE INTO THE OIL.

8. ALLOW TO FRY FOR 3-4 MINUTES.

9. TURN THEM HALF WAY THROUGH TO ENSURE THEY ARE EVENLY BROWN.

10. ONCE COOKED, SCOOP THEM OUT OF THE OIL USING A SLOTTED SPOON AND ALLOW OIL TO DRAIN.

11. SERVE KOOSE WITH KOKO AND GROUNDNUT.

1. WASH KONTOMIRE LEAVES WITH ENOUGH WATER.

2. CUT KONTOMIRE INTO DESIRED STRIPES.

3. PUT THE CUT KONTOMIRE INTO SAUCEPAN WITH LITTLE WATER AND PLACE ON HIGH HEAT.

4. COVER AND BRING TO BOIL.

5. TURN THE KONTOMIRE AFTER ABOUT 5MINS OF COOKING TO MAKE SURE EVERYTHING IS COOKED THROUGH.

6. TURN OFF FIRE AND SET ASIDE.

7. BLEND ONIONS, TOMATOES, PEPPER.

8. POUR PALM OIL INTO A SAUCEPAN, ADD THE REMAINING SLICED ONIONS AND MOMONI (SALTED FISH).

9. FRY TILL ONIONS ARE SOFTENED. ADD THE BLENDED MIXTURE. BRING TO SIMMER ON MEDIUM HEAT.

10. ADD FISH AND SALT AND ALLOW TO COOK FOR 5 TO 7 MINS.

11. GENTLY STIR IN THE STEAMED KONTOMIRE.

12. LET SIMMER FOR ANOTHER 5MINS AFTER THE KONTOMIRE HAS BEEN ADDED.

13. READY TO SERVE KONTONMIRE STEW WITH AMPESI OR RICE.

1. STEAM FISH OR MEAT WITH GARLIC, GINGER AND ONIONS IN A SAUCEPAN.

2. ADD TOMATOES PASTE.

3. BOIL GARDEN EGGS, PEPPER AND TOMATOES AND BOIL FOR ABOUT 5MINS.

4. BLEND ALL THE GARDEN EGGS, PEPPER AND TOMATOES AFTER BOILED AND ADD TO THE SAUCEPAN.

5. ADD WATER TO BRING THE SOUP TO ITS DESIRED THICKNESS. ADD SALT AND CUBES TO TASTE.

6. ALLOW THE SOUP TO SIMMER FOR ABOUT 30 -45MINS.

7. LIGHT SOUP IS READY TO BE SERVED WITH FUFU.

1. CUT YAM TUBER INTO ABOUT 4 PARTS. PLACE IT ON CUTTING BOARD AND PEEL THE SKIN OFF.
2. CHOP THE PEELED YAM INTO SMALL SIZES.
3. RINSE YAM THOROUGHLY TO ENSURE THERE IS NO DIRT.
4. TRANSFER RINSED YAM INTO A COOKING POT AND FILL IT WITH WATER.
5. PLACE IT ON HIGH HEAT.
6. ADD THE TOMATOES, ONIONS, AND PEPPER TO THE YAM.
7. COVER IT AND ALLOW IT TO BOIL.
8. TRANSFER FISH INTO A CLEAN BOWL.
9. REMOVE TOMATOES, ONION AND PEPPER FROM THE BOILING PAN AND TRANSFER INTO A BLENDER.
10. ADD FISH.
11. ADD SALT TO TASTE.
12. USING A SPATULA, MASH THE YAM AGAINST THE SIDES OF THE COOKING POT TO GET A PORRIDGE CONSISTENCY.
13. ADD PALM OIL.
14. ALLOW IT TO BOIL FOR ABOUT 7–10MINS.
15. PUT OFF THE FIRE AND SERVE WHILES HOT.

1. RINSE CORN KERNEL WITH WATER IN A LARGE BOWL 2-3 TIMES UNTIL WATER RUNS CLEAR.

2. ADD TWO CUPS OF WATER TO THE BOWL AND LEAVE TO SOAK OVERNIGHT.

3. DRAIN WATER FROM THE CORN.

4. MAKE A MIXTURE WITH CORNMEAL AND WATER.

5. STRAIN MIXTURE AND ADD TO CORN PORRIDGE.

6. ADD SALT AND COOK FOR 10 MINS.

7. ENJOY OBLAYO WITH SUGAR, MILK AND GROUNDNUT.

STEPS FOR OKRO SOUP

1. WASH CHOPPED MEAT, CRABS, AND COWHIDE IN A LARGE BOWL.

2. WASH AND CUT INTO PIECES 1 ONION, GARLIC, GINGER AND PEPPER. BLEND UNTIL SMOOTH.

3. PLACE MEAT, CRABS, AND COWHIDE (WELE) IN A SAUCEPAN, ADD A LITTLE WATER AND BRING TO A BOIL.

4. POUR IN BLENDED INGREDIENTS AND STEAM FOR ABOUT 10MINS UNTIL TENDER.

5. IN A SEPARATE POT, PLACE CHOPPED OKRO, ADD A CUP OF WATER AND LET IT SIMMER FOR ABOUT 8MIMS. REMOVE FROM FIRE AND ALLOW IT TO COOL.

6. NOW POUR SOME PALM OIL INTO ANOTHER SAUCEPAN ADD SALTED FISH AND ONIONS TO COOK FOR ABOUT 3MINS.

7. ADD RESERVED BLENDED KPAKPO SHITO (PEPPER), GINGER AND GARLIC AND ALLOW IT TO SIMMER FOR AN 5MINS.

8. WASH AND CHOP TOMATOES AND ADD TO THE SAUCE.

9. ADD YOUR STEAMED CRAB.

10. NOW ADD YOUR STEAMED BEEF AND COWHIDE AND LEAVE IT FOR ABOUT 2MINS.

11. ADD YOUR COOKED OKRO AND STIR TO MIX EVENLY REDUCE THE HEAT AND ALLOW IT COOK FOR ABOUT 10MINS. DD SOME SALT TO YOUR PREFERRED TASTE.

12. OKRO SOUP IS READY TO BE SERVED WITH BANKU OR KOKONTE.

1. RINSE THE RICE AND PUT IT IN A MEDIUM COOKING POT.

2   ADD WATER AND SALT TO TASTE.

3. PUT RICE IN HIGH HEAT AND BRING TO BOIL.

4. AFTER A WHILE LESSEN THE HEAT TO MEDIUM.

5. ALLOW COOKING TILL ALL WATER IS ABSORBED AND THE RICE IS VERY SOFT.

6. TURN OFF THE HEAT.

7. AFTER THAT, USE A WOODEN LADDLE TO MASH THE RICE AGAINST THE SIDES OF THE POT INTO BALLS RENDERING TO BE REQUIRED SERVING.

8. SERVE OMO TUO [RICE BALLS] WITH SOUP OF CHOICE.

STEPS FOR PALAVER SAUCE

1. SOAK MELON SEEDS (AGUSHI) IN WATER.
2. WASH KONTOMIRE LEAVES WITH ENOUGH WATER.
3. CUT KONTOMIRE INTO DESIRED STRIPES.
4. PUT THE CUT KONTOMIRE INTO SAUCEPAN WITH LITTLE WATER AND PLACE IN HIGH HEAT.
5. COVER AND BRING TO BOIL.
6. TURN THE KONTOMIRE AFTER ABOUT 5MINS OF COOKING TO MAKE SURE EVERYTHING IS COOKED THROUGH.
7. TURN OFF FIRE AND SET ASIDE.
8. BLEND ONION, TOMATOES, PEPPER, GARLIC, GINGER AND SET ASIDE.
9. WASH AGUSHI AND BLEND.
10. ALSO SLICE THE REMAINING ONIONS.
11. POUR PALM OIL INTO A SAUCEPAN, ADD THE REMAINING SLICED ONIONS AND MOMONI (SALTED FISH).
12. FRY TILL ONIONS ARE SOFTENED. ADD THE BLENDED MIXTURE. BRING TO SIMMER ON MEDIUM HEAT. ADD FISH AND SALT AND ALLOW TO COOK FOR 5 TO 7MINS.
13. ADD THE BLENDED EGUSHI .DO NOT STIR, COVER AND ALLOW TO SIMMER FOR 8 TO 10MINS.
14. GENTLY STIR IN THE STEAMED KONTOMIRE.
15. LET SIMMER FOR ANOTHER 5MINS AFTER THE KONTOMIRE HAS BEEN ADDED.
16. READY TO SERVE PALAVER SAUCE WITH RICE OR AMPESI

STEPS FOR PALM-NUT SOUP

1. BLEND THE ONION, GARLIC AND GINGER.

2. IN A LARGE SAUCEPAN, TRANSFER MEAT, BLENDED ONION, GARLIC, GINGER, SALT AND OTHER SPICES TO TASTE.

3. STEAM MEAT OVER MEDIUM HEAT AND ADD PALM NUT PASTE (FIRST POUND PALM FRUIT WHICH HAS BEEN BOILED TOGETHER WITH ADDING SOME AMOUNT OF WATER IN OTHER TO OBTAIN A PALM PASTE).

4. ADD WATER DEPENDING ON THE THICKNESS YOU WANT (ADD PEPPER, FRESH TOMATOES AND ONIONS).

5. STIR YOUR PEPPER, FRESH TOMATOES AND ONIONS. REMOVE FROM SOUP AND BLEND UNTIL SMOOTH.

6. ADD THE TOMATOES MIXTURE TO THE SOUP AND STIR.

7. ADD YOUR SMOKED FISH AND "PREKESE" AND ALLOW TO COOK.

8. ENJOY PALM NUT SOUP WITH FUFU, BANKU OR KOKONTE.

1. RINSE THE RICE.

2. BRING THE WATER TO A BOIL. ONCE IT'S BOILING, ADD A PINCH OF SALT.

3. MAINTAIN A SIMMER.

4. COOK WITHOUT STIRRING.

5. FLUFF THE RICE WITH A FORK.

6. RICE IS READY TO BE SERVED WITH YOUR DESIRED SAUCE.

STEPS FOR ROASTED CORN
(CORN ON THE COB)

1. HEAT UP THE CHARCOAL FIRE OR GRILL THEN PLACE THE CORN OVER THE HEAT TO TOAST.

2. BREAK THE COCONUT INTO PIECES AND WASH IN SALT SOLUTION.

3. ONCE THE CORN ARE PROPERLY ROASTED AND GOLDEN COLOR IN APPEARANCE, BRING OUT FROM HEAT.

4. SERVE THE ROASTED CORN WITH COCONUT.

STEPS FOR ROASTED PLANTAIN

1. REMOVE THE PEEL AND SLICE THE PLANTAIN ON AN ANGLE ¼ INCH SLICES.

2. PLACE THE PLANTAIN ON THE GRILL.

3. KEEP TURNING IT UNTIL ALL SIDES ARE WELL COOKED.

4. BAKE UNTIL GOLDEN BROWN.

5. SERVE ROASTED PLANTAIN WITH GROUNDNUT.

1. CLEAN THE SOBOLO LEAVES.

2. IN A LARGE SAUCEPAN, POUR THE SOBOLO LEAVES AND ADD WATER TO COVER UP THE LEAVES.

3. UNDER HIGH HEAT PUT MIXTURE ON FIRE.

4. WASH AND PEEL AND CHOP PINEAPPLE AND GINGER.

5. ADD THE GINGER AND CLOVES TO THE SOBOLO LEAVES ON FIRE.

6. USING A SIEVE OR COLANDER, DRAIN AND SEPARATE THE LIQUID FROM THE REST OF THE MIXTURE AND SET ASIDE.

7. BLEND THE FRESH PINEAPPLE UNTIL SMOOTH.

8. MIX THE SOBOLO JUICE WITH THE BLENDED PINEAPPLE.

9. ALLOW THE DRINK TO COOL DOWN COMPLETELY.

10. ADD SUGAR TO TASTE.

11. SERVE NATURAL REFRESHING SOBOLO OVER ICE.

STEPS FOR TOMATO STEW

1. WASH AND CHOP PEPPER, TOMATOES, ONIONS, OTHER VEGETABLES.

2. BLEND THE INGREDIENTS UNTIL SMOOTH.

3. HEAT-UP OIL IN A SAUCEPAN.

4. ADD SLICE OF ONION AND ALLOW TO FRY UNTIL IT TURNS GOLDEN BROWN.

5. ADD THE BLENDED MIXTURE.

6. ADD TOMATO PASTE AND STIR TO ALLOW IT MIX PROPERLY.

7. ADD SPICES AND VEGETABLES.

8. ADD CHOICE OF FISH OR STEAMED MEAT AND ALLOW TO COOK.

9. REDUCE HEAT AND ALLOW TO SIMMER.

10. SERVE TOMATO STEW WITH RICE OR AMPESI.

STEPS FOR TUO ZAAFI (TZ)

1. BOIL ENOUGH WATER AND ADD CORN-FLOUR TO COOK AS PORRIDGE.

2. FETCH SOME OF THE PORRIDGE AND SET ASIDE IN A SEPARATE BOWL.

3. MIX DRY CORN AND CASSAVA FLOUR (KOKONTE) AND ADD MIXTURE TO THE BOILING PORRIDGE ON FIRE BIT BY BIT.

4. STIR CONTINUOUSLY AND THOROUGHLY TO AVOID LUMPS USING A SPATULA.

5. CONTINUE STIRRING UNTIL TUO-ZAAFI IS WELL COOKED.

6. MOULD IT INTO SERVING BOWLS.

7. SERVE WITH AYOYO SOUP AND STEW.

STEPS FOR WAAKYE (RICE AND BEANS)

1. WASH THE BEANS AND SOAK THEM IN WATER FOR 3-4 HOURS.

2. DRAIN THE BEANS AND PUT THEM IN A LARGE SAUCEPAN WITH PARTLY FILLED WITH WATER. LEAVE TO COOK FOR 45MINS.

3. WASH THE SORGHUM LEAVES AND CUT 3-4 INCHES, ADD TO THE BOILING BEANS AND COOK TOGETHER.

4. IF THE SORGHUM LEAVES ARE NOT ACCESSIBLE, SUBSTITUTE WITH A TEASPOON OF BAKING SODA TO GIVE WAAKYE ITS DISTINCTIVE COLOR.

5. AFTER 5MINS, REMOVE THE SORGHUM LEAVES FROM THE POT.

6. WASH THE RICE THOROUGHLY AND ADD TO THE BEANS. AND ADD MORE WATER TO THE POT.

7. COOK THE MIXTURE FOR 15-20MINS.

8. MAKE SURE THE FOOD DOES NOT BURN. STIR OCCASIONALLY WHILES IT'S COOKING.

9. SEASON WITH SALT.

10. YOU CAN SERVE WAAKYE WITH SHITO, FISH, EGG, GARI, SPAGHETTI, AND FRIED PLANTAIN.

STEPS FOR YOKE GARI (COOKED BEANS)

1. RINSE AND SORT BEANS TO REMOVE THE BAD ONES.

2. POUR BEANS INSIDE A POT, ADD WATER AND PUT IT ON FIRE TO BOIL FOR ABOUT 1 HOUR.

3. ADD SALT TO TASTE.

4. ONCE BEANS BECOMES TENDER, AND SET IT ASIDE.

5. ADD YOUR CHOPPED ONIONS, 1 SALTED FISH (MOMONI) INTO THE HOT OIL AND LET IT FRY TILL IT BECOMES GOLDEN BROWN.

6. SERVE YOKE GARI WITH PALM OIL AND FRIED PLANTAIN.